SUPER CUTE PAPER -DIY-

Head

Arms

Right Left

Body

A   B

dewmuffins

Birds

Happy   Sad

When you miss your friend

Me   You

SUPER CUTE PAPER TOYS
-DIY-

Copyright © 2016 Instituto Monsa de Ediciones

Editor, concept, and project director
Anna Minguet

Art director, design and layout
Eva Minguet
(Monsa Publications)

Cover design
Eva Minguet
(Monsa Publications)

INSTITUTO MONSA DE EDICIONES
Gravina 43 (08930)
Sant Adrià de Besòs
Barcelona (Spain)
Tlf. +34 93 381 00 50
www.monsa.com
monsa@monsa.com

Visit our official online store!
www.monsashop.com

Follow us on facebook!
facebook.com/monsashop

ISBN: 978-84-16500-29-1
D.L. B 14881-2016
Printed by Grafilur

SUPER CUTE PAPER TOYS
-DIY-

monsa

INTRO

The DIY phenomenon is growing, and at the hand of expert artists in the world of illustration and papercraft, we managed to gather 38 printed templates of excellent quality on couché paper of 200 gr, with which to create fabulous toys.

We find all kinds of figures, always with a simple pattern, designed with all kinds of details, creating different reliefs to simulate volume and give more realism to our toys, accomplishing a true work of art.

The papercraft or paper toys are a fun and creative activity covering an endless number of projects.
The creation process is different for each artist, starting from an initial sketch, which later can be scanned and printed, cut, folded and glued, thus creating our "exclusive Paper Toy!"

El fenómeno DIY sigue creciendo, y de la mano de los mejores artistas del mundo de la ilustración y del papercraft hemos conseguido reunir 38 plantillas impresas con una excelente calidad, en papel couché de 200 gr, con las que poder crear fabulosos muñecos.

Encontraremos todo tipo de figuras siempre con un patrón sencillo, diseñados con todo tipo de detalle, creando diferentes relieves para simular volumen y dar más realismo a nuestros muñecos haciendo una obra de arte de cada uno de ellos.

Los papercraft o paper toys son una actividad entretenida y creativa que abarcan un sinfín de proyectos.
El proceso de creación es diferente según cada artista, partiendo de un boceto inicial, que más tarde se puede digitalizar e imprimir, cortar, doblar y pegar, creando de esta manera nuestro "exclusivo Paper Toy!".

INDEX OF DESIGNERS

ANDREA INNOCENT

www.andreainnocent.com
www.otoshimono.org

Andrea Innocent is a Melbourne-based professional illustrator and designer. She started her career in fashion and textiles, before moving into photography, animation and interactive media. Represented by The Jacky Winter Group since 2007 and with 15 years experience creating commercial work, she has built up an impressive list of clients including Microsoft, Cambridge University Press, NBN, Libra Hearts, Toyota Corolla, Cadbury Australia, Rolling Stone Magazine, Nylon Magazine US, The Age, Weekend Australia Magazine, Clemenger BBDO and many others.

Andrea is often called upon for high concept work that communicates big ideas. Her range of skills in conceptual development, illustration and animation including brand identities, print campaigns, web based projects and digital publishing put her in high demand. Andrea regularly speaks as an industry authority at events such as Melbourne Museum's Top Designs and AGIDEAS, covering topics surrounding design, illustration and the creative life. Her spare time is spent wrangling a baby and a corgi, sometimes in that order.

Andrea Innocent es una diseñadora e ilustradora profesional que vive en Melbourne. Comenzó su carrera en la industria de la moda, y de ahí pasó a la fotografía, la animación y la comunicación interactiva. Representada por el Jacky Winter Group desde 2007 y con 15 años de experiencia, se ha hecho con una impresionante lista de clientes entre los que figuran Microsoft, Cambridge University Press, NBN, Libra Hearts, Toyota Corolla, Cadbury Australia, Rolling Stone Magazine, Nylon Magazine US, The Age, Weekend Australia Magazine, Clemenger BBDO y muchos otros.

A menudo, se solicitan sus servicios para desarrollar nuevos conceptos destinados a transmitir grandes ideas. Sus conocimientos en desarrollo conceptual, ilustración, animación, branding, publicidad, proyectos para web y publicaciones digitales, hace que sus servicios estén muy solicitados. Andrea participa en charlas regularmente como una autoridad de la industria, eventos como Top Designs y AGIDEAS de Melbourne Museum, abarcando temas sobre diseño, ilustración, la vida creativa. Su tiempo libre lo dedica a reñir a su bebé y a su perro corgi, a menudo en este orden.

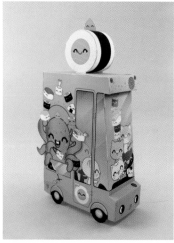

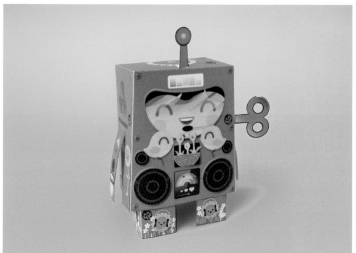

DEWMUFFINS

www.dewmuffins.com
www.instagram.com/dewmuffins

Our world is filled with delightful characters and creatures ready to embark on amazing, magical, extraordinary and adventurous journeys.

We were hit by the paper toy bug several years ago when designers starting applying their unique illustrative styles to paper templates.

Another attraction is that paper toys are very inexpensive to make which makes them accessible to a wide audience, and special tools are not required. Within an hour or two you have a beautiful 3 dimensional work of art.

Nuestro mundo está lleno de deliciosas criaturas y personajes listos para embarcarse en un asombroso, mágico, extraordinario e intrépido viaje.

Nos picó el virus de los paper toys hace unos años cuando los diseñadores comenzaron a aplicar sus ilustraciones en plantillas de papel.

Nos vimos atraídos por este tipo de juguetes porque son económicos, lo cual los hace accesibles a mucha gente, y además, no se necesitan instrumentos especiales. En un par de horas o tres de trabajo, se puede realizar una pieza artística en tres dimensiones.

NAOSHI

www.nao-shi.com
www.facebook.com/naoshi.sunae

Naoshi is a Japanese artist whose distinctive characters and original style are recognized around the world. She uses shiny colorful sand, called Sunae in Japan, to create surreal people living in the real world. In her effort to familiarize more people with Sunae outside of Japan, she has participated in a wide range of projects including gallery exhibitions, commercial work, and children's workshops.

Naoshi es una artista japonesa cuyos personajes y estilo son reconocidos en todo el mundo.
Para crear sus personajes, utiliza la técnica japonesa llamada Sunae, que consiste en dar color a la arena blanca, consiguiendo todo tipo de matices y brillos.
Naoshi se esfuerza por dar a conocer el Sunae al público, participando en una gran cantidad de proyectos, entre los que se incluyen exposiciones, trabajos comerciales y tiendas de niños.

SAMANTHA EYNON

www.samanthaeynon.com
twitter.com/samanthaeynon
www.instagram.com/samanthaeynon
https://www.etsy.com/uk/shop/SamanthaEynon

Samantha Eynon is an Illustrator and Designer based in the Midlands in the UK. She is a lover of vintage, cute and colourful things, and can often be found rummaging around charity shops for anything with a bright, bold pattern.

Her aim is simple, to create things that make people, smile!

Samantha Eynon es una ilustradora y diseñadora que vive en el centro de Inglaterra. Le encantan las antigüedades, las cosas bonitas y coloridas, y a menudo se la puede ver revolviendo en las tiendas de caridad en busca de cualquier objeto que tenga un diseño brillante y original.

Su ambición es simple, ¡el crear objetos que hagan sonreír a la gente!

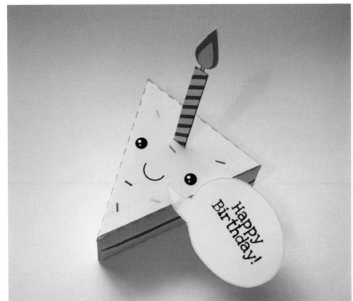

TOXIC PAPER FACTORY

VICENÇ LLETÍ ALARTE

www.toxicpaperfactory.com
www.behance.net/toxicpaperfactory
twitter.com/toxic_procyon

What he likes most is the creation of new creatures. Give them personality, feelings, character and try to make them real beings. Graduated in Graphic Design in 2011, he has developed his personal work from its own brand, Toxic Paper Factory, where he exhibits his creatures in the form of illustrations and papertoys. His papertoys are characterized by spherical structures and a tender and adorable appearance.

Lo que más le gusta hacer y a lo que dedica todo el tiempo que puede, es la creación de nuevas criaturas. Otorgarles personalidad, sentimientos y carácter y hacer que se vuelvan seres reales. Diplomado en diseño gráfico en 2011 ha desarrollado su trabajo personal desde su propia marca, Toxic Paper Factory, donde expone sus criaturas en forma de ilustraciones y papertoys. Sus papertoys se caracterizan por tener estructuras esféricas y un aspecto tierno y adorable.

TOUGUI

www.tougui.fr
www.instagram.com/tougui
twitter.com/tougui1
www.behance.net/tougui

Guillaume aka Tougui is a French freelance graphic designer and Papertoy maker based in Annecy.
His work is influenced by street art, cartoon's of 50's and board culture.
No depression, his works always speak about ironical stuff and sweet dreams.
His universe is populated by funny landscape, funky characters and fresh colors.
He is always on the lookout for new mediums.

Guillaume, alias Tougui, es un diseñador gráfico y de juguetes de papel que vive en Annecy.
Su obra está influenciada por el street art, los dibujos animados de los años 50 y la cultura del surf. La depresión no existe, sus obras hablan siempre de cosas irónicas y sueños agradables. Su universo está poblado de paisajes divertidos, personajes de moda y colores frescos.
Siempre está atento a cualquier nueva tendencia.

TARA HANDMADE

www.tarahandmade.com
www.etsy.com/shop/TaraHandmade

Tara Handmade consists of Anna and Gerard, a couple of designers from Barcelona.
Anna loves to create dolls and accessories for home decoration, crafts and sewing. Gerard is passionate about graphic design and interiorism, and he takes care of creating paper toys when not working on his graphic design studio.

Both began to create gadgets and papertoys from Tara Handmade when their first daughter Àstrid was born. Since she was a baby, Àstrid's room was filled with papertoys and other handmade items. Although she is still young to cut and paste papertoys, her parents do not stop creating new designs for both children and adults, who still like to play and have fun like kids.

Tara Handmade está formado por Anna y Gerard, una pareja de diseñadores de Barcelona.
A Anna le encanta crear muñecos y accesorios para decorar la casa, hacer manualidades y coser. A Gerard le apasiona el diseño gráfico, y el interiorismo, y él se encarga de crear los papertoys cuando no está trabajando en su estudio de diseño gráfico.

Los dos empezaron a crear los juguetes y paper toys de Tara Handmade cuando nació su primera hija, Àstrid. Desde que era un bebé, su habitación se llenó de papertoys y demás artículos hechos a mano. Aunque ella todavía es pequeña para recortar y pegar los muñecos de papel, sus papás no dejan de crear nuevos diseños, tanto para niños como para adultos a los que todavía les gusta jugar y disfrutar como niños.

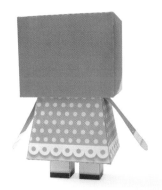

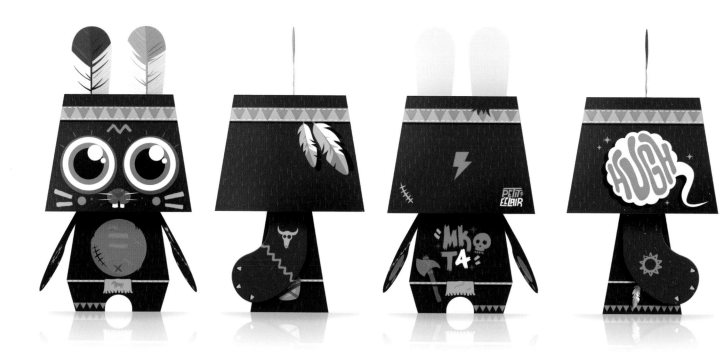

www.mkt4.com

Born in Auvergne, France, Laëtitia Dugat aka MKT4 currently lives and works as an illustrator and painter in Clermont-Ferrand. At an early age, during her life in the rural territories of Combrailles, she developed an interest and a specific sensibility for country, farm animals and colors of nature, that will be the matrix of her creativity as an artist. After graduating from Cournon High School (Arts appliqués), she obtained a BTEC Higher National Diploma in visual communication (Chaumont), and a BA in Art History at Montpellier University.

Her artistic work is influenced by Kawaii Japanese art, and based on a very coloured universe including essentially animal figures that make her creations highly recognizable from others. Being open to different paths and art forms, she expresses herself through various supports: exclusive birth announcement cards, thank-you cards, multiple format paintings (including on wood), screen-prints, mural frescoes, collages and so on. She collaborated especially with famous sport brands like "Salomon" or "Clothing Co.", and realized wall paintings in French public hospitals like the CHU Estaing. Laëtitia's main activity remains editorial illustration through regular partnerships with Fleurus editions, Turbulences presses and Mango.

Nacida en Auvergne, Francia, Laëtitia Dugat alias MKT4, vive en Clermont-Ferrand en donde ejerce como ilustradora y pintora. Desde su más tierna infancia, cuando vivía en una zona rural de Combraillles, se sintió atraída y desarrolló una sensibilidad especial hacia todo lo relacionado con el campo, la granja, los animales y los colores de la naturaleza. Ello se convirtió en la piedra angular de sus creaciones artísticas. Después de graduarse en la Cournon High School (artes plásticas), obtuvo un BTEC (Higher National Diploma) en comunicación visual (Chaumont) y un BA en Historia del Arte de la Universidad de Montpellier.

Su obra artística está muy influenciada por el arte Kawaii japonés, se basa en un universo muy colorista que incluye esencialmente figuras de animales, dando un estilo fácilmente reconocible con respecto a otros. Siempre abierta a otros caminos y formas artísticas, le gusta expresarse a través de varios soportes: tarjetas de felicitación y agradecimiento, pinturas de diferentes formatos (incluyendo la madera), serigrafía, frescos, collages, etc. Ha colaborado con marcas famosas como "Salomon" or "Clothing Co.", y ha realizado pinturas murales para hospitales públicos como el Centro Hospitalario Universitario Estaing. Su principal actividad sigue siendo la ilustración editorial a través de las colaboraciones con ediciones Fleurus, Turbulences y Mango.

ZEROLABOR

Zsolt Papp aka Zerolabor, is a Hungarian graphic designer and art director, who currently lives in Miami, making a living with his wife and three kids.
He started making paper toys around 2008. Zerolabor's characters, are simple, with a strong physiognomy.

Zsolt Papp alias Zerolabor es un diseñador gráfico y director artístico húngaro, que vive en Miami con su mujer y sus tres niños.
Empezó haciendo juguetes de papel en torno a 2008. Sus personajes son simples y con una fisonomía fuerte.

PUK-PUK

www.pukpuk.cz

In the works of PUK-PUK duo, there has always been a place for illustrations and characters of weird godlings, daemons, magical beings and made up superheroes.

After they had explored the world of paper toys, they were pleased to send their characters around the world so that anyone can put them together and exhibit them at home. The theme of their paper toys is interconnectivity with global and local aspects. The artists live in the area of vivid, traditional culture with a lot of folk costumes and ornaments. They like connecting local influences to characters of different cultures and religions.

En las obras de PUK-PUK duo, siempre ha habido un lugar para ilustraciones y personajes basados en seres mágicos, dioses menores, demonios y superhéroes ficticios.

Tras haber explorado el mundo de los paper toys, decidieron compartirlos con sus seguidores, para que pudieran disfrutarlos desde sus casas. El principal concepto de sus paper toys es la interconectividad con aspectos globales y locales, lo intenso, la cultura tradicional con costumbres folclóricas. Estos artistas tratan de conectar con sus trabajos diferentes influencias de cualquier cultura o religión.

INDEX OF TEMPLATES

Doolçot

Kami Kokeshi

Blue Doll

Toxic Ketsue Kigata

Billy

Chat

Krou Magnon

Renard

Petit Éclair

Panda

Fula

Maneki

Carla & Chacha

Purple Doll

Tita

Red Doll

Shiba-Inu Dog

Green Doll

Cosmonaut

THE LITTLE KING

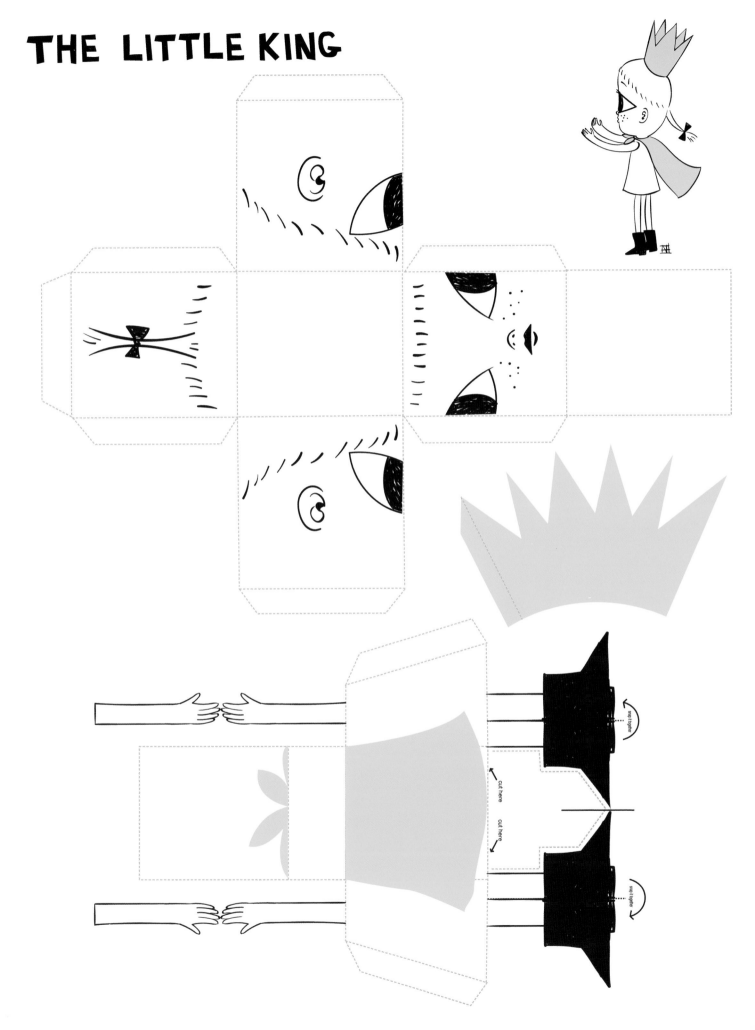

NEKO
TERIBI

cut around legs

cut around legs

cut here

cut here

tail

swap it together

swap it together

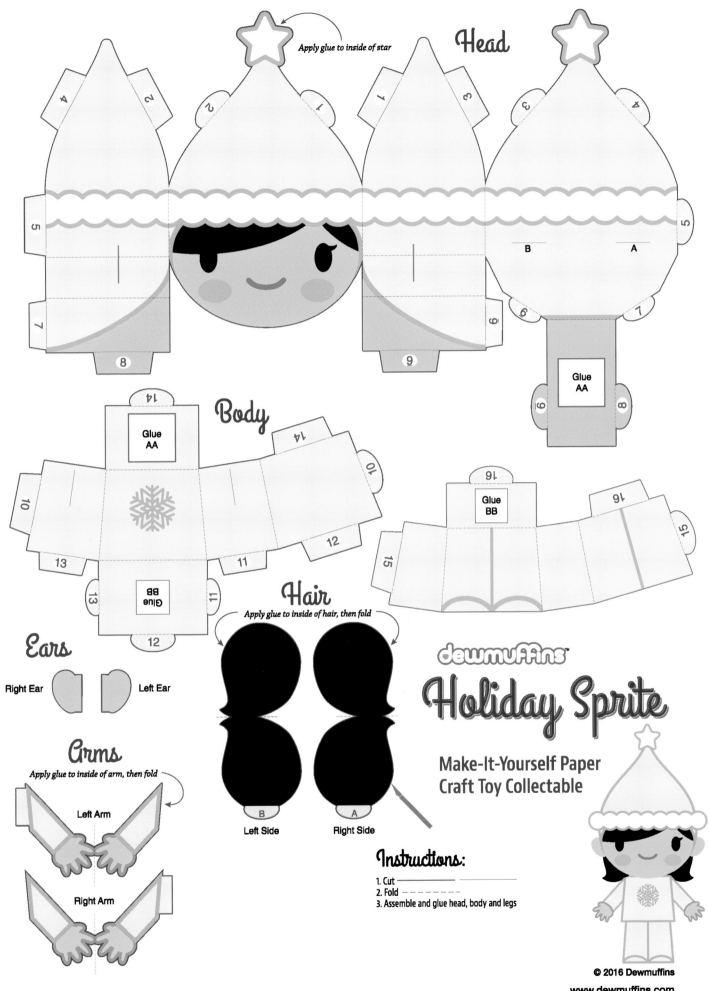

Valentine's

Together or apart, you remain in my heart

Two friendship paper toys. One for you and one to share with your special friend.

This one belongs to your **Friend**

Head

Arms
Right   Left

Birds
Happy   Sad

When you miss your friend

Body
A   B   dewmuffins

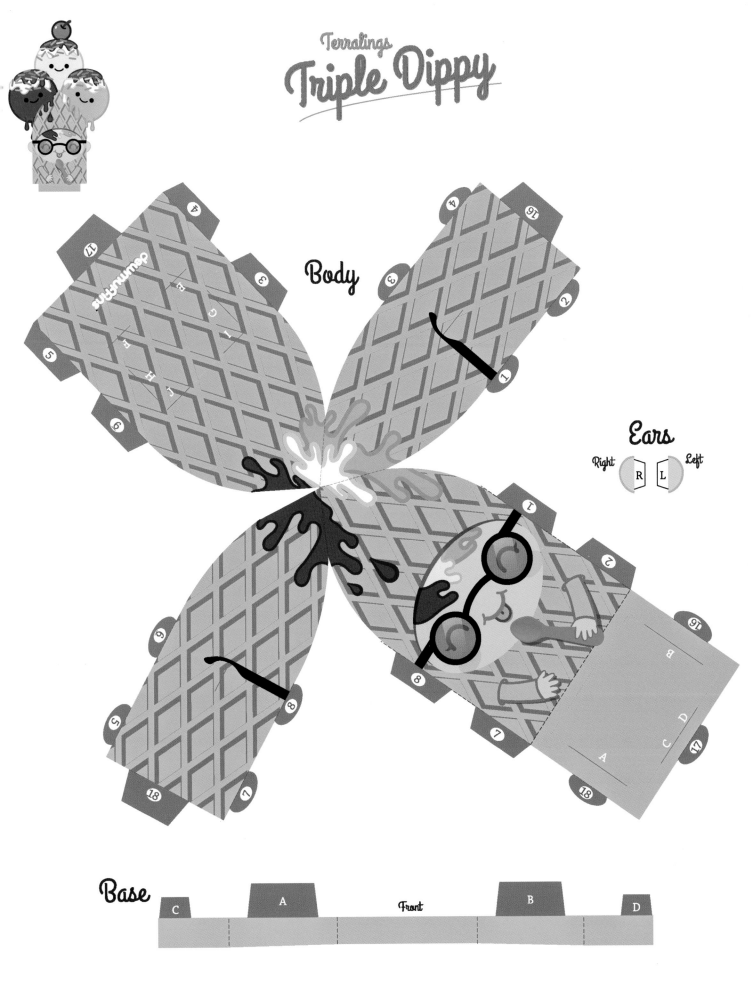

Terratings

Triple Dippy

Body

Ears

Right R L Left

Base

C   A   Front   B   D

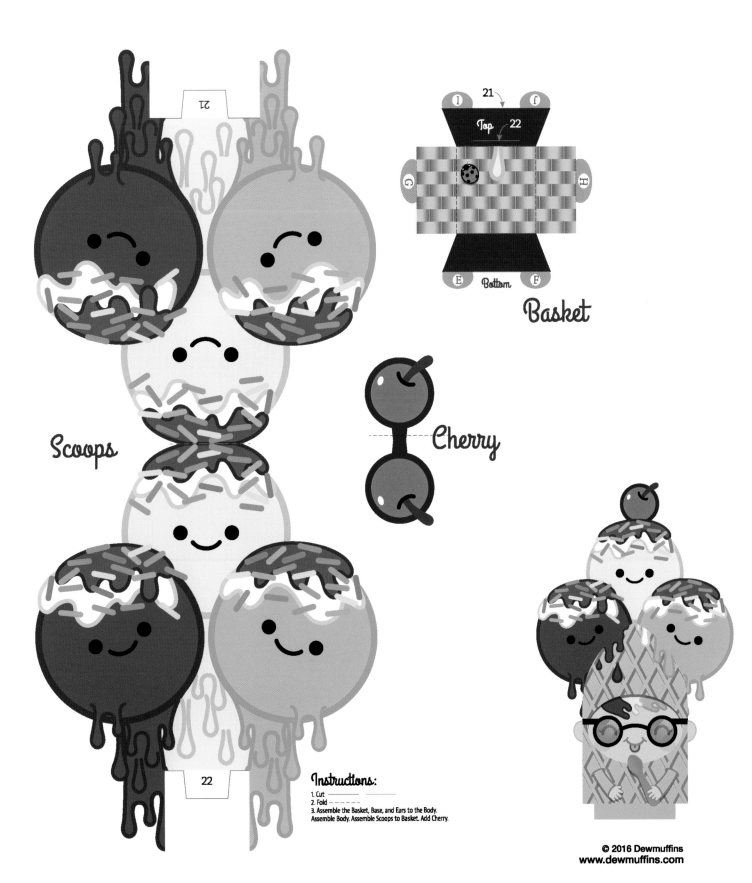

Scoops

Basket

Cherry

Instructions:
1. Cut ——————
2. Fold - - - - - -
3. Assemble the Basket, Base, and Ears to the Body.
Assemble Body. Assemble Scoops to Basket. Add Cherry.

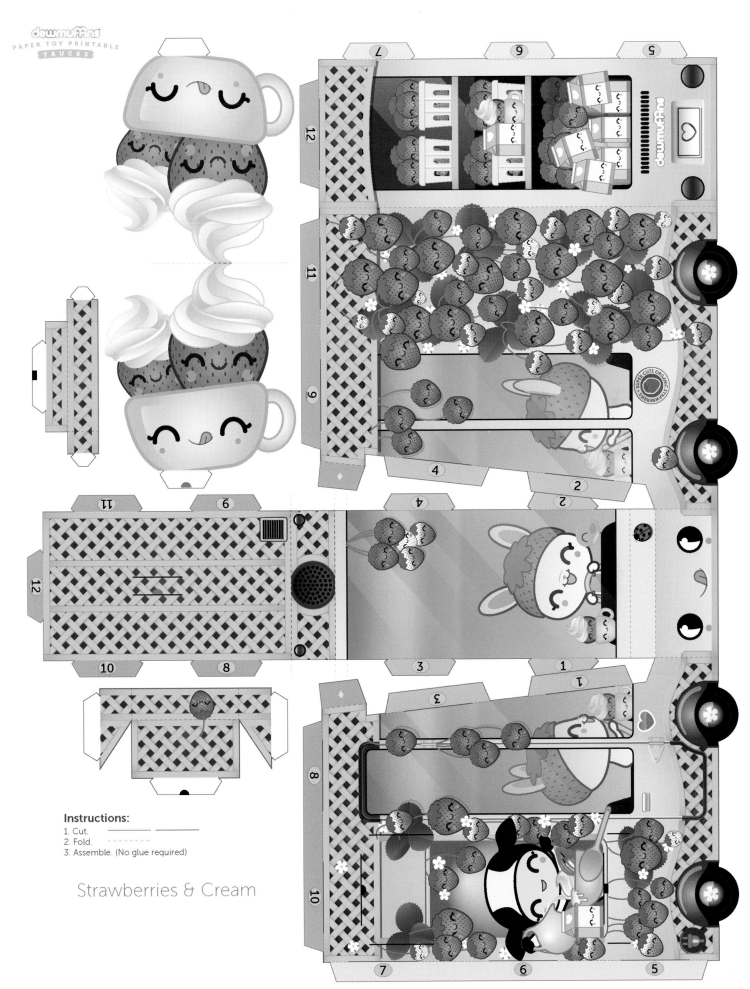

Strawberries & Cream

Instructions:
1. Cut.
2. Fold.
3. Assemble. (No glue required)

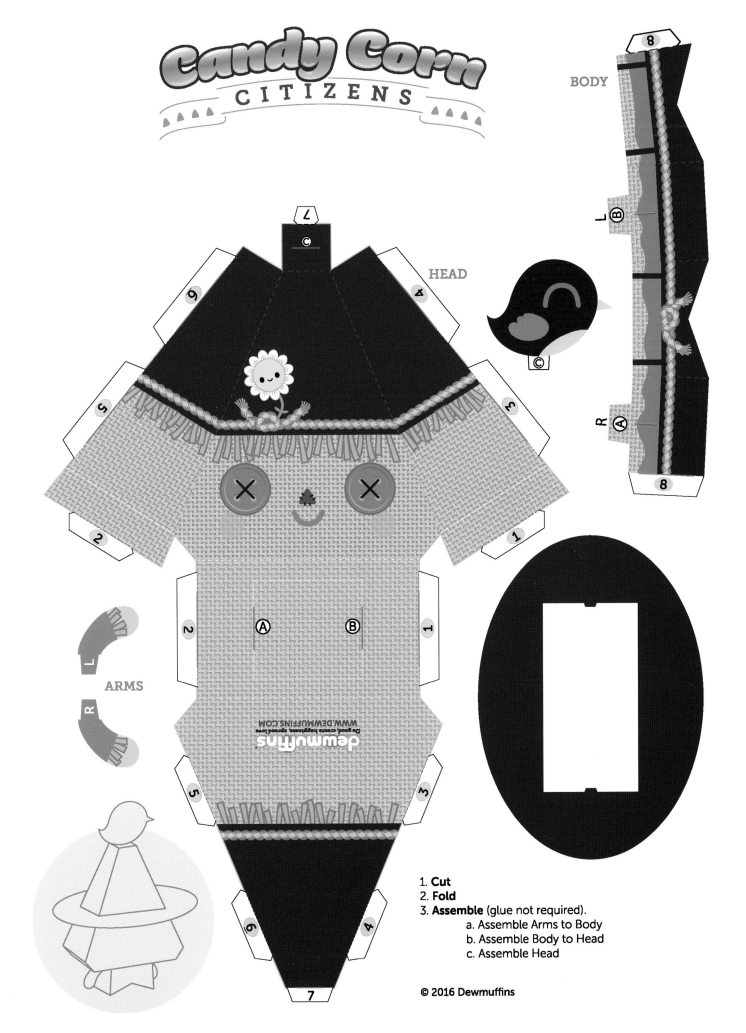

Candy Corn CITIZENS

BODY

HEAD

ARMS

Do good, create happiness, spread love
WWW.DEWMUFFINS.COM
dewmuffins

1. **Cut**
2. **Fold**
3. **Assemble** (glue not required).
    a. Assemble Arms to Body
    b. Assemble Body to Head
    c. Assemble Head

© 2016 Dewmuffins

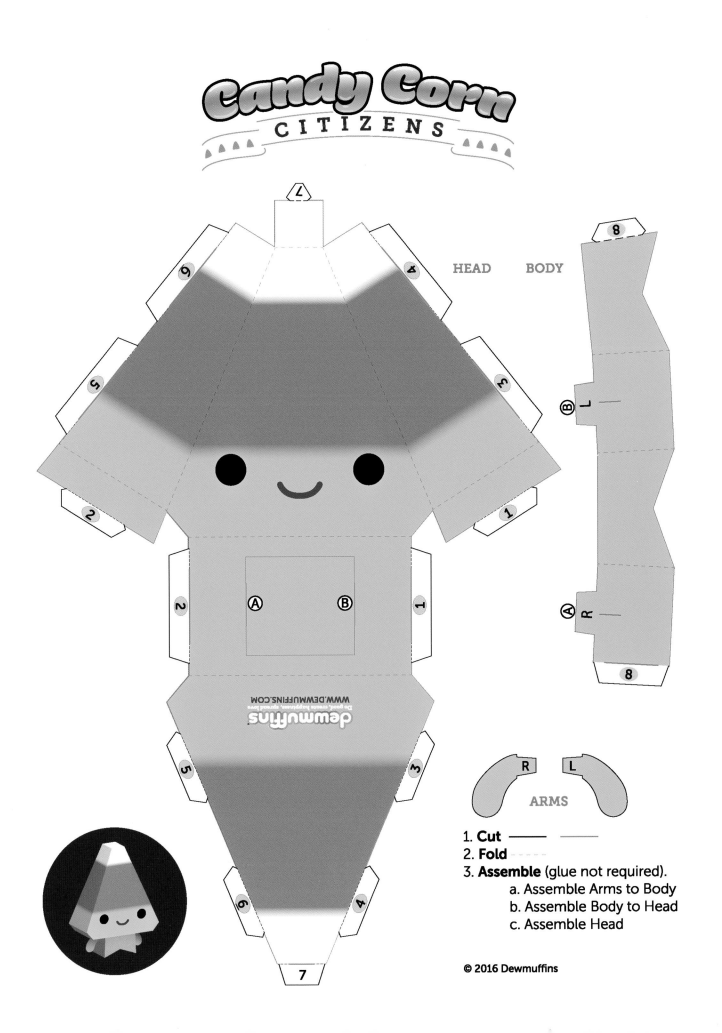

Candy Corn
CITIZENS

HEAD   BODY

dewmuffins
Do good, create happiness, spread love
WWW.DEWMUFFINS.COM

ARMS

1. **Cut** ——————
2. **Fold** - - - - - -
3. **Assemble** (glue not required).
    a. Assemble Arms to Body
    b. Assemble Body to Head
    c. Assemble Head

© 2016 Dewmuffins

Candy Girl
Designed by Naoshi

Cut

✂— Cut
- - - - Fold
💧 Glue

http://www.nao-shi.com

A PIECE OF CAKE!

—— Cut

--- Score

HAPPY BIRTHDAY!

www.samanthaeynon.com

FOR MY CUPCAKE!

—— Cut

- - - Score

Blank for your own message!

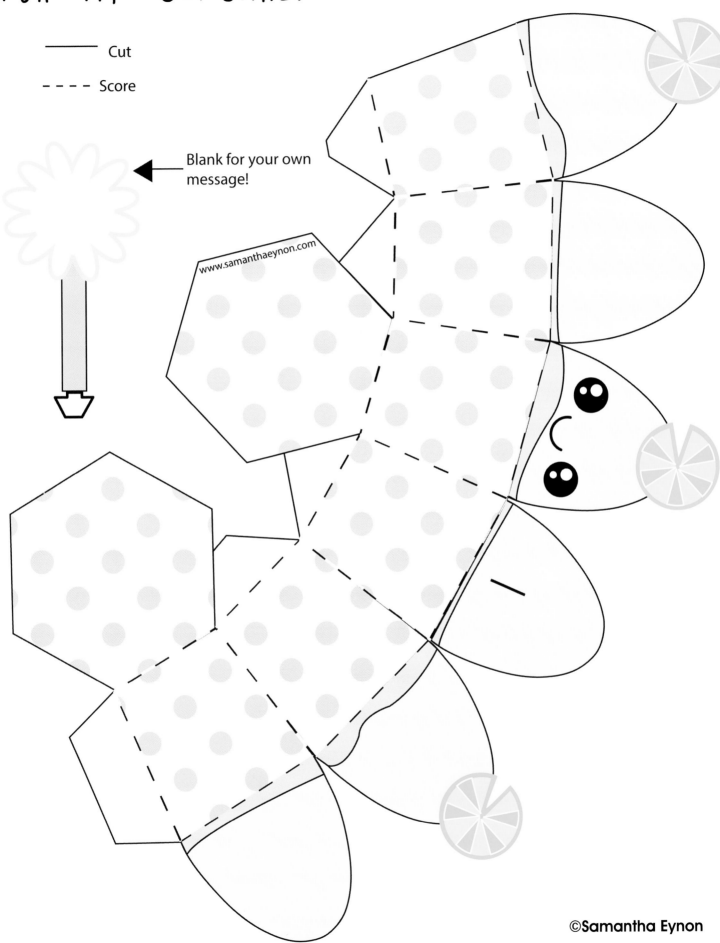

www.samanthaeynon.com

BARRY AMOR

Cut along solid lines, score and fold dashed line.

Assemble as shown in image of finished toy

Stick assembled quiver on back of body

Stick feet to underside of body

Arms go in slots on side of body

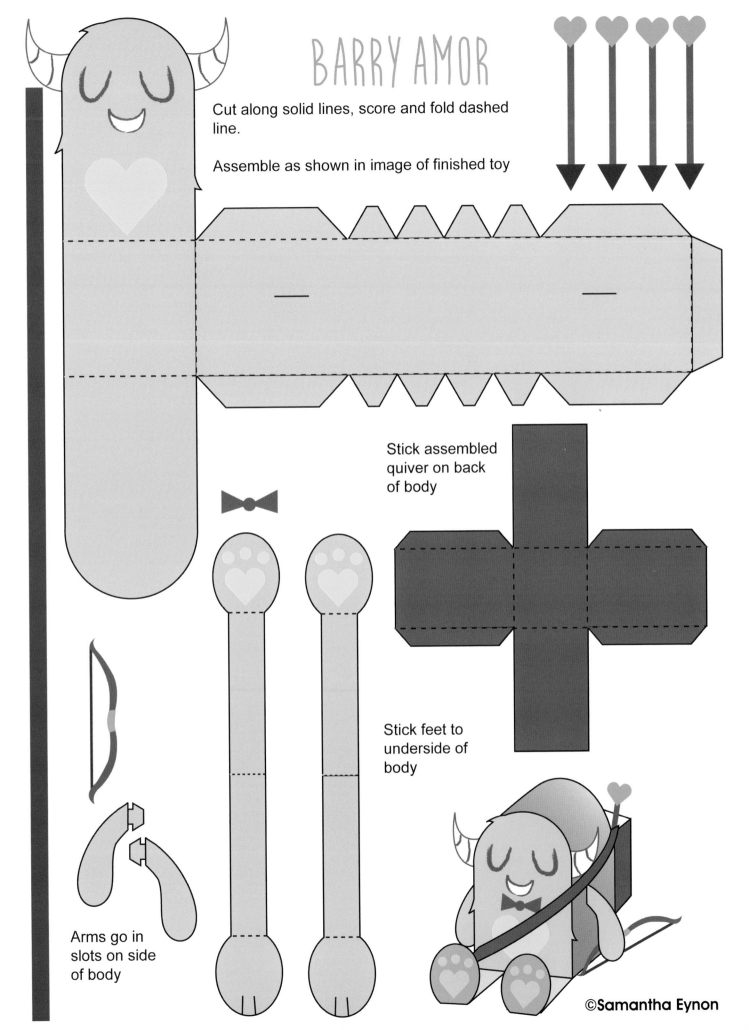

GEORGE THE CAT

Cut along solid lines, score and bend along dashed lines

Fold and stick back to back

Cut round ears and fold upright

To Mum

Tail goes in slot at back of model

Blank envelope to address yourself and stick to paw

stick arms back to back then put in side slots

Stick back to back and stick to paw

©Samantha Eynon

chuchutai

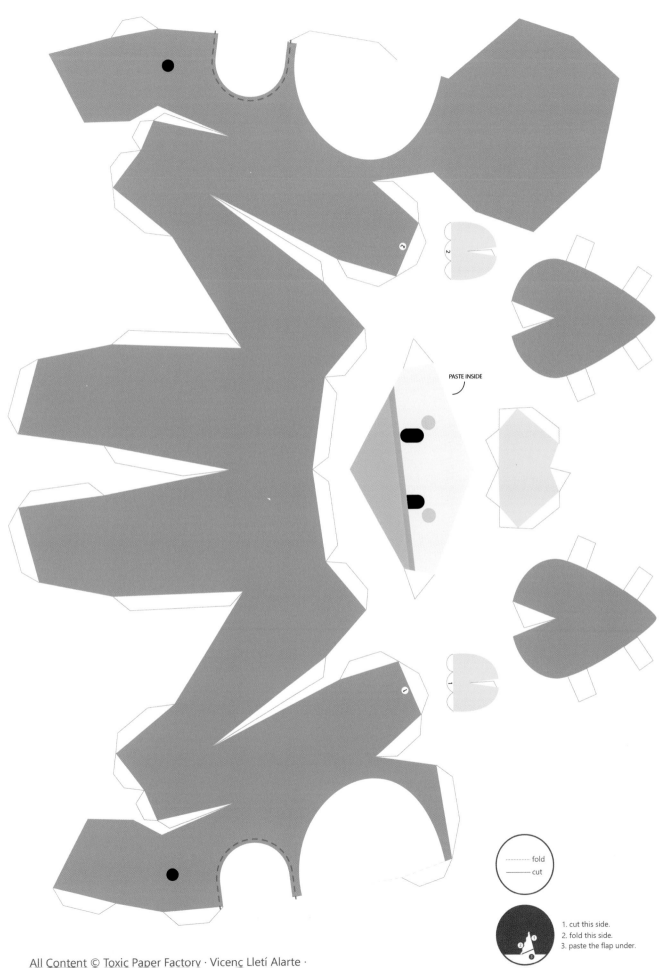

PASTE INSIDE

fold
cut

1. cut this side.
2. fold this side.
3. paste the flap under.

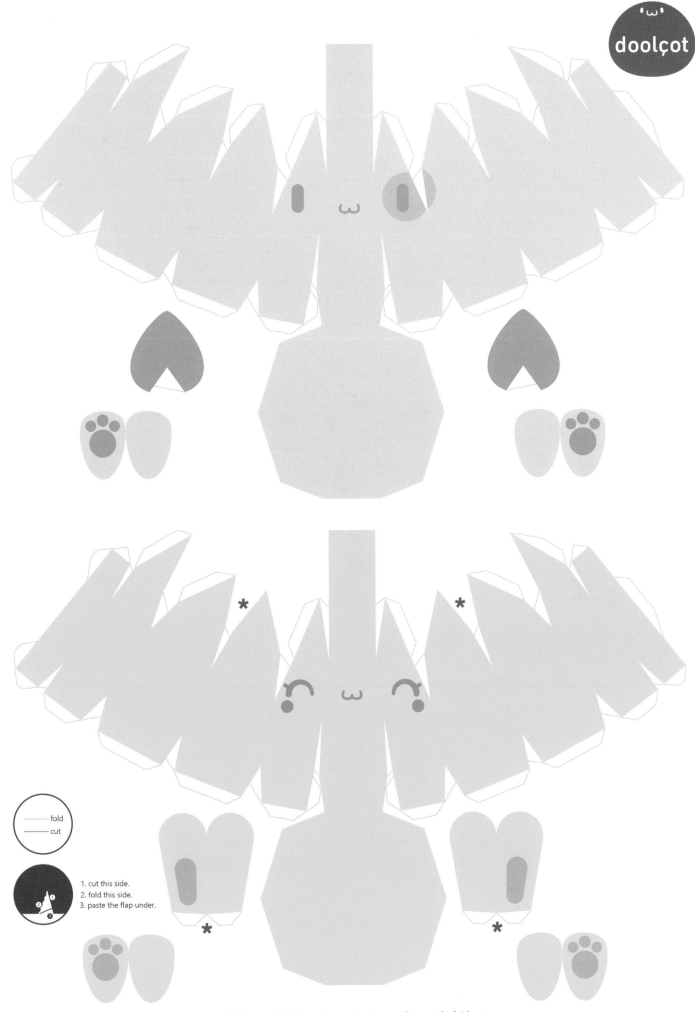

doolçot

fold
cut

1. cut this side.
2. fold this side.
3. paste the flap under.

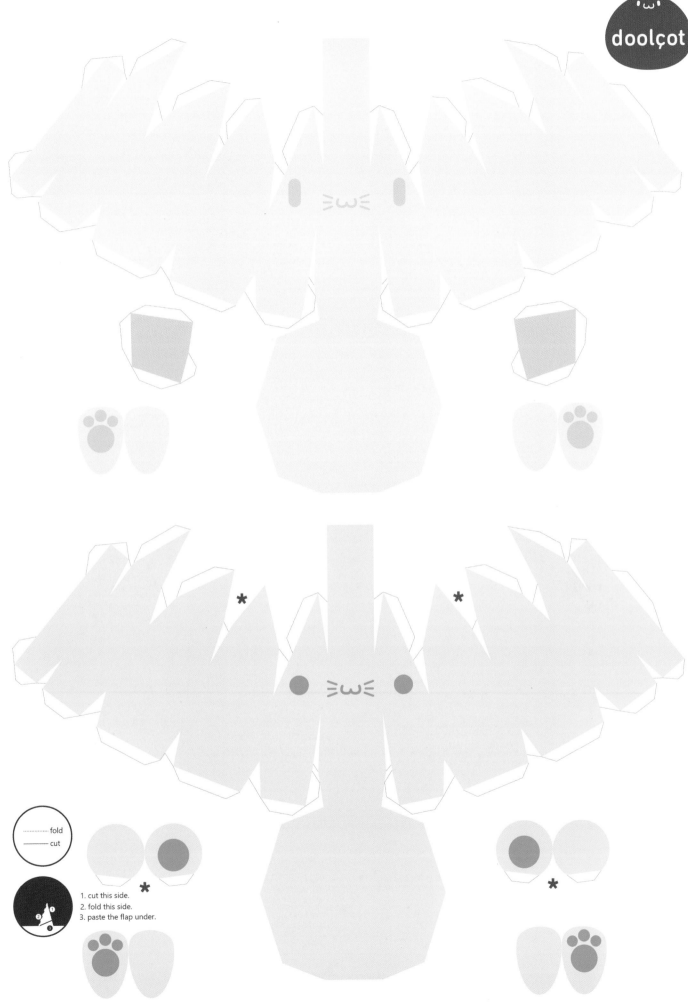

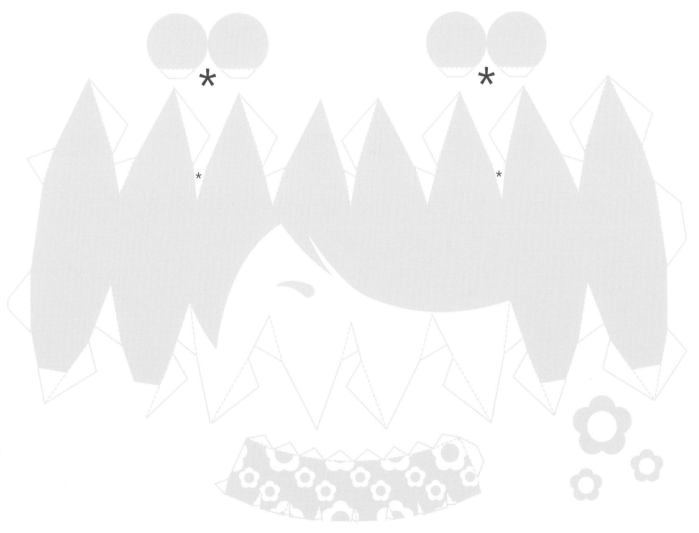

.... fold
———— cut

1. cut this side.
2. fold this side.
3. paste the flap under.

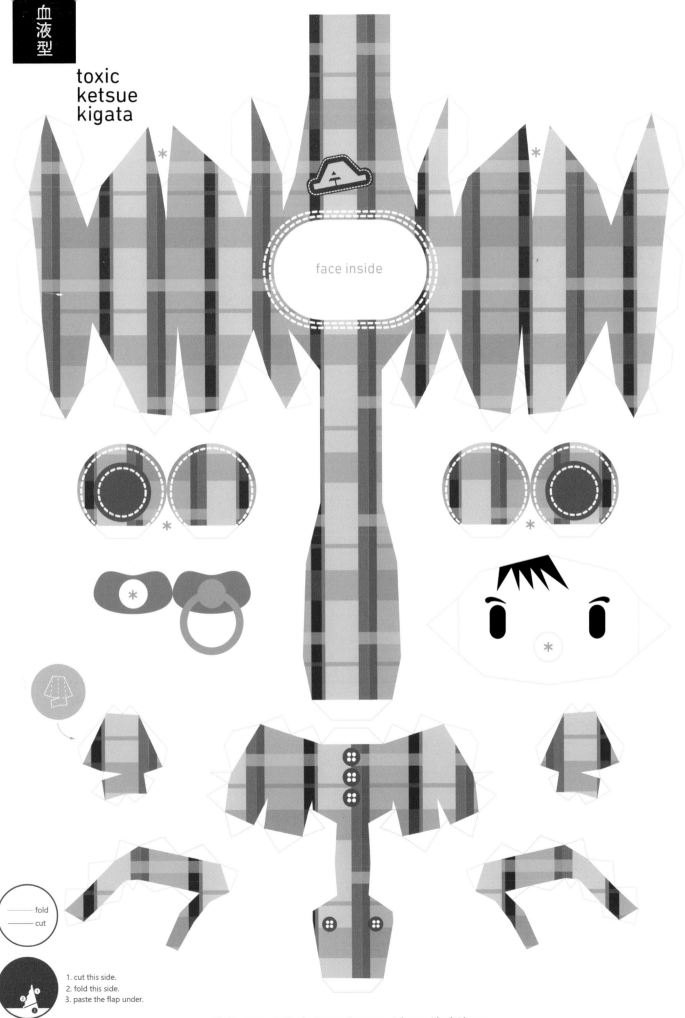

血液型

toxic
ketsue
kigata

face inside

fold
cut

1. cut this side.
2. fold this side.
3. paste the flap under.

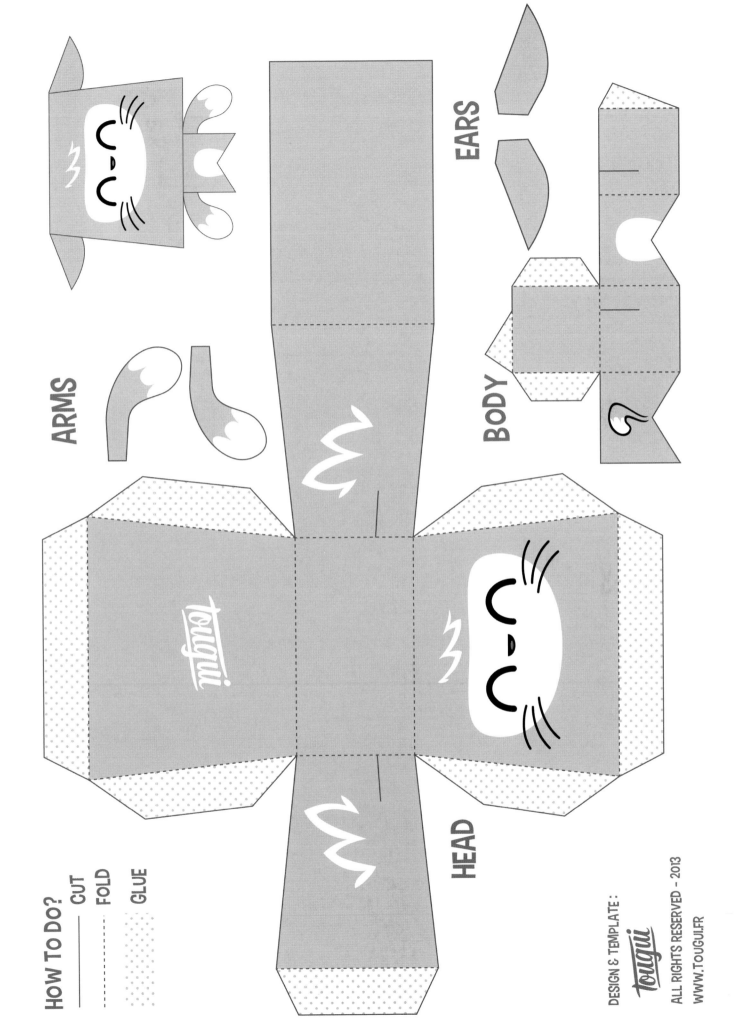

EARS

ARMS

BODY

HEAD

HOW TO DO?
— CUT
------ FOLD
······ GLUE

DESIGN & TEMPLATE :

tougui

ALL RIGHTS RESERVED – 2013
WWW.TOUGUI.FR

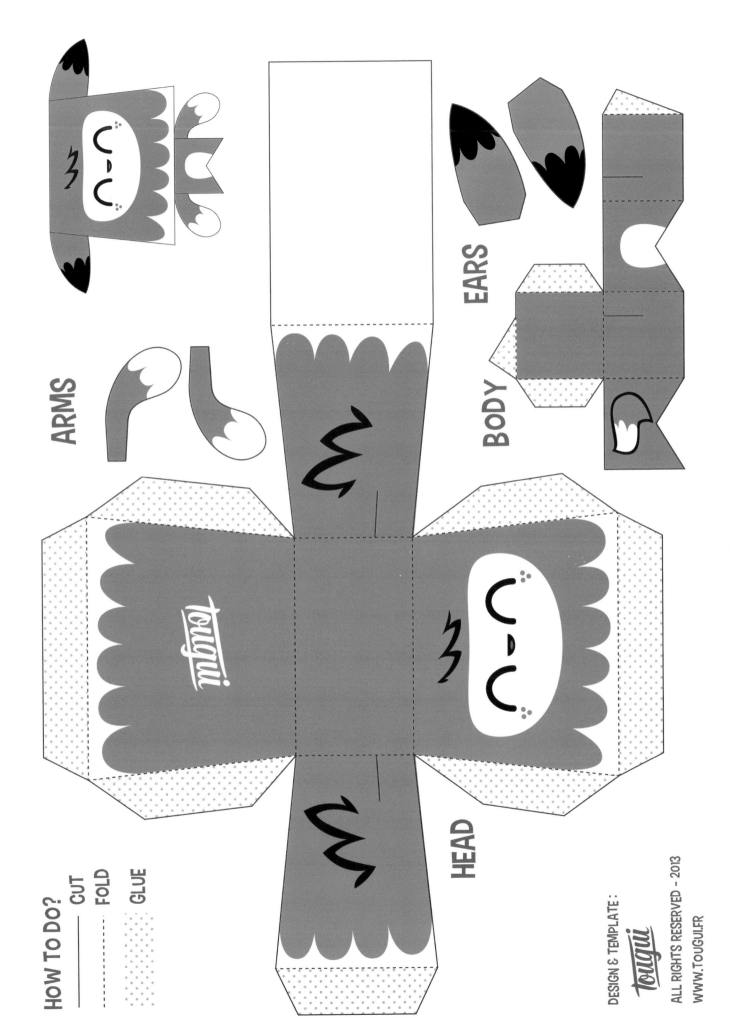

ARMS

EARS

BODY

HEAD

Tougui

DESIGN & TEMPLATE :
Tougui

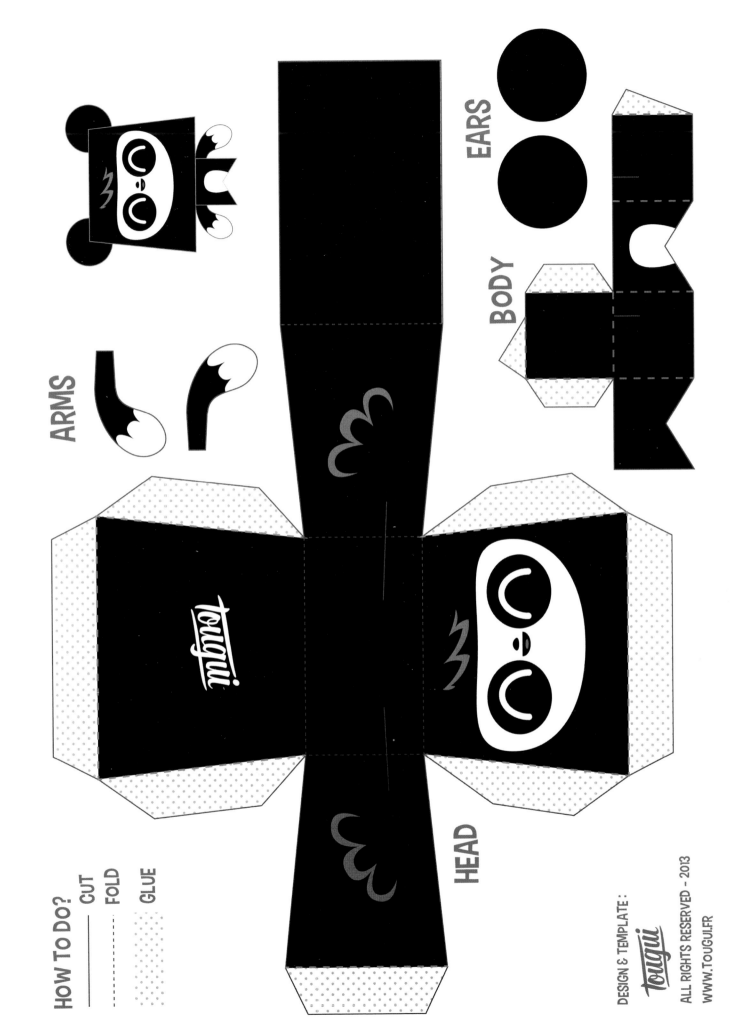

EARS

BODY

ARMS

HEAD

tougui

HOW TO DO?

——— CUT

- - - - - FOLD

:::::::: GLUE

BAG

ARM

ARM

BODY

tougui

EARS

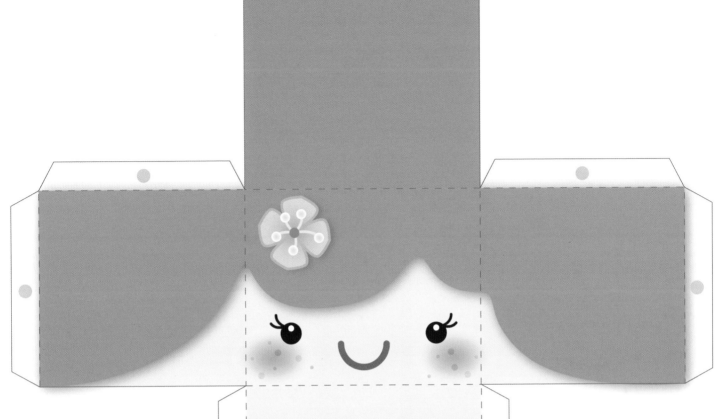

01
PURPLE
DOLL

*Cut all the continuous lines and
fold the discontinuous lines.
Glue along the tabs marked with
grey circle.
Match the numbers and glue them
together.*

TARA^{hu} *dolls*

e-mail
info@tarahandmade.com
web
www.tarahandmade.com
shop on-line
www.etsy.com/shop/tarahandmade

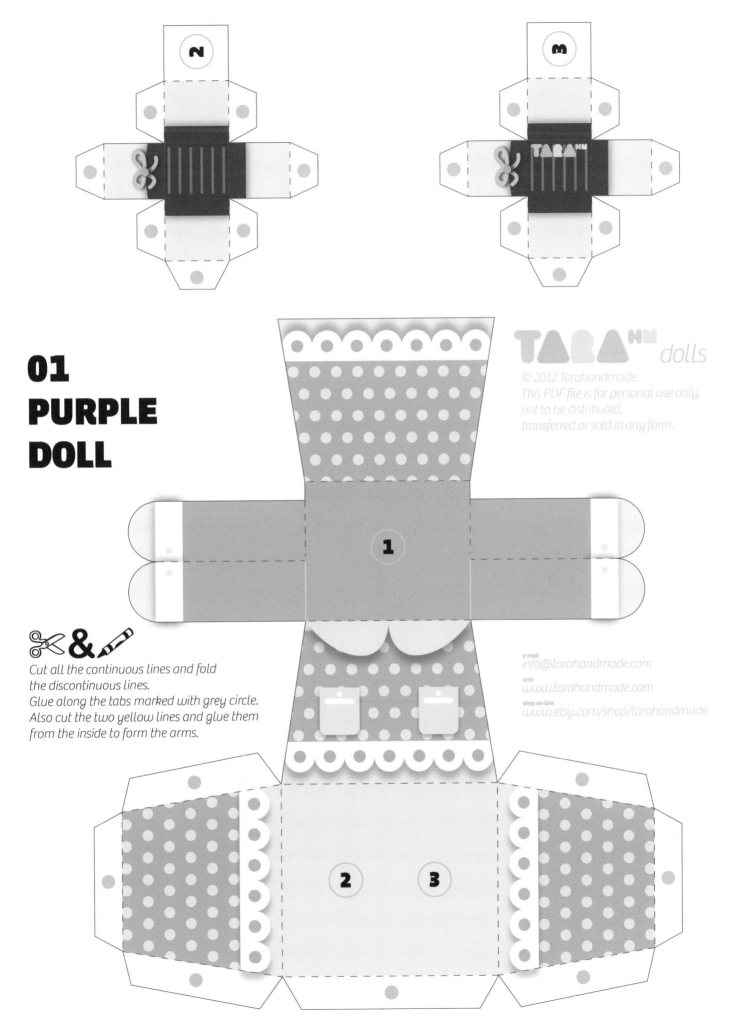

01 PURPLE DOLL

TABA™ dolls

Cut all the continuous lines and fold
the discontinuous lines.
Glue along the tabs marked with grey circle.
Also cut the two yellow lines and glue them
from the inside to form the arms.

e-mail
info@tarahandmade.com
web
www.tarahandmade.com
shop on-line
www.etsy.com/shop/tarahandmade

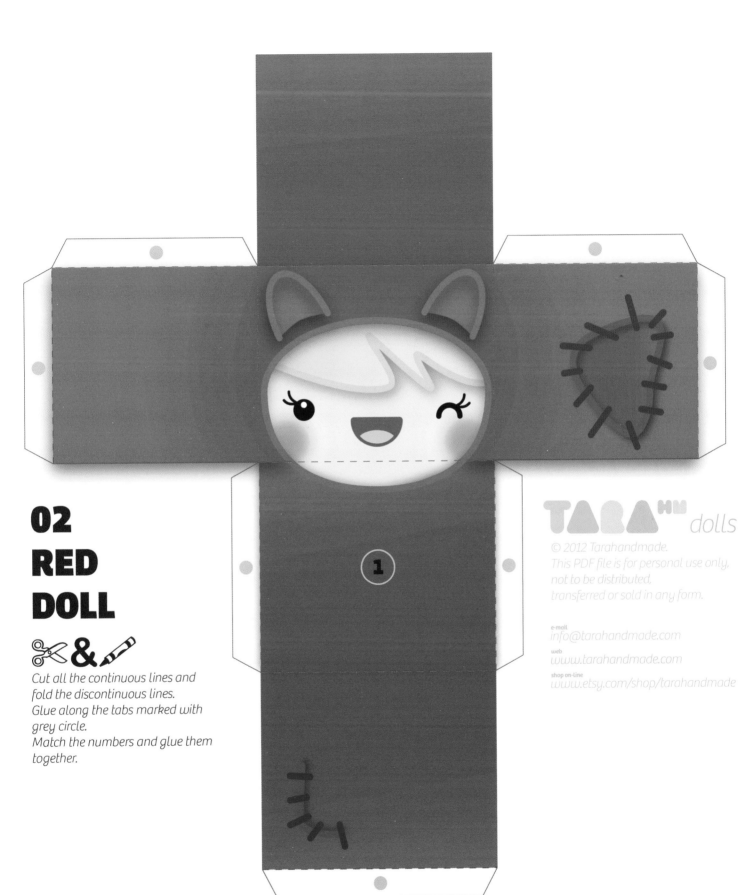

02
RED
DOLL

Cut all the continuous lines and fold the discontinuous lines.
Glue along the tabs marked with grey circle.
Match the numbers and glue them together.

TARA ᴴᴹ *dolls*

e-mail
info@tarahandmade.com
web
www.tarahandmade.com
shop on-line
www.etsy.com/shop/tarahandmade

1

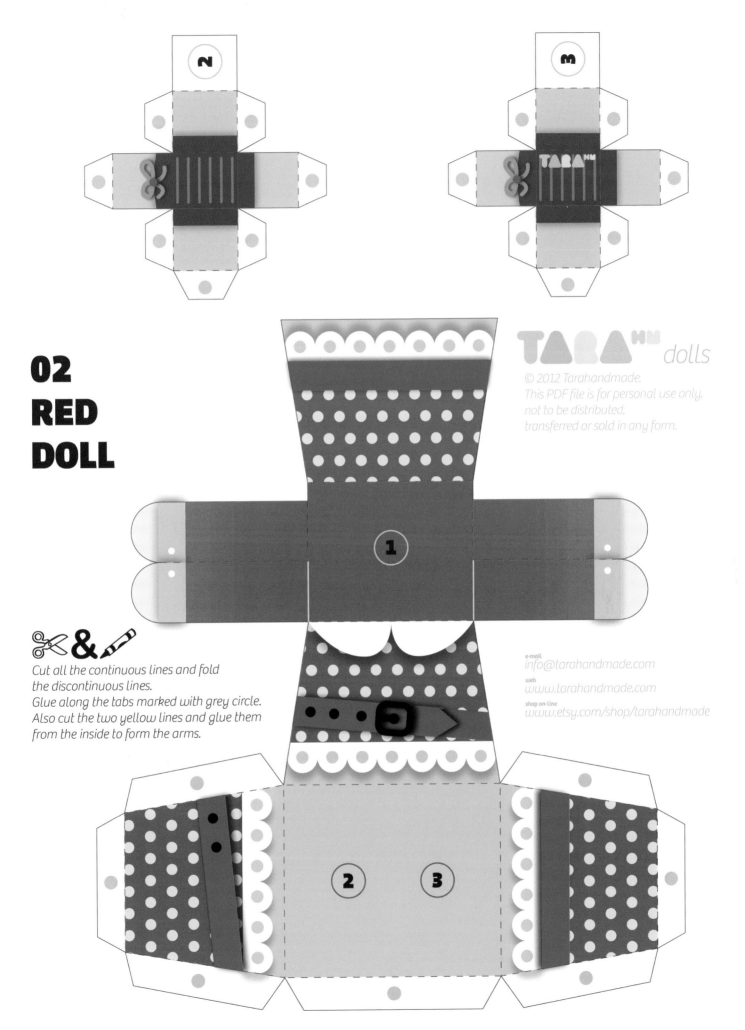

02 RED DOLL

Cut all the continuous lines and fold the discontinuous lines.
Glue along the tabs marked with grey circle.
Also cut the two yellow lines and glue them from the inside to form the arms.

e-mail
info@tarahandmade.com
web
www.tarahandmade.com
shop on-line
www.etsy.com/shop/tarahandmade

TARA ᴴᴹ dolls

03 GREEN DOLL

Cut all the continuous lines and fold the discontinuous lines.
Glue along the tabs marked with grey circle.
Match the numbers and glue them together.

TARA HM *dolls*

e-mail
info@tarahandmade.com
web
www.tarahandmade.com
shop on-line
www.etsy.com/shop/tarahandmade

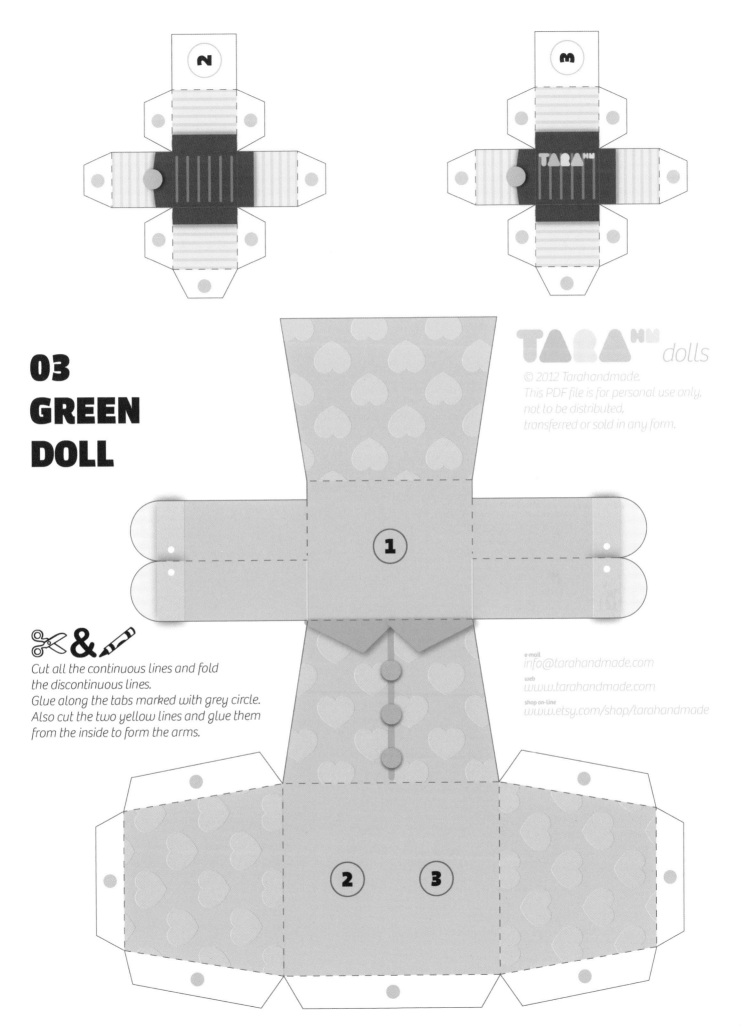

03 GREEN DOLL

TARA™ *dolls*

Cut all the continuous lines and fold
the discontinuous lines.
Glue along the tabs marked with grey circle.
Also cut the two yellow lines and glue them
from the inside to form the arms.

e-mail
info@tarahandmade.com
web
www.tarahandmade.com
shop on-line
www.etsy.com/shop/tarahandmade

04
BLUE
DOLL

✂ & 🖍

Cut all the continuous lines and fold the discontinuous lines. Glue along the tabs marked with grey circle. Match the numbers and glue them together.

TARA HM *dolls*

e-mail
info@tarahandmade.com
web
www.tarahandmade.com
shop on-line
www.etsy.com/shop/tarahandmade

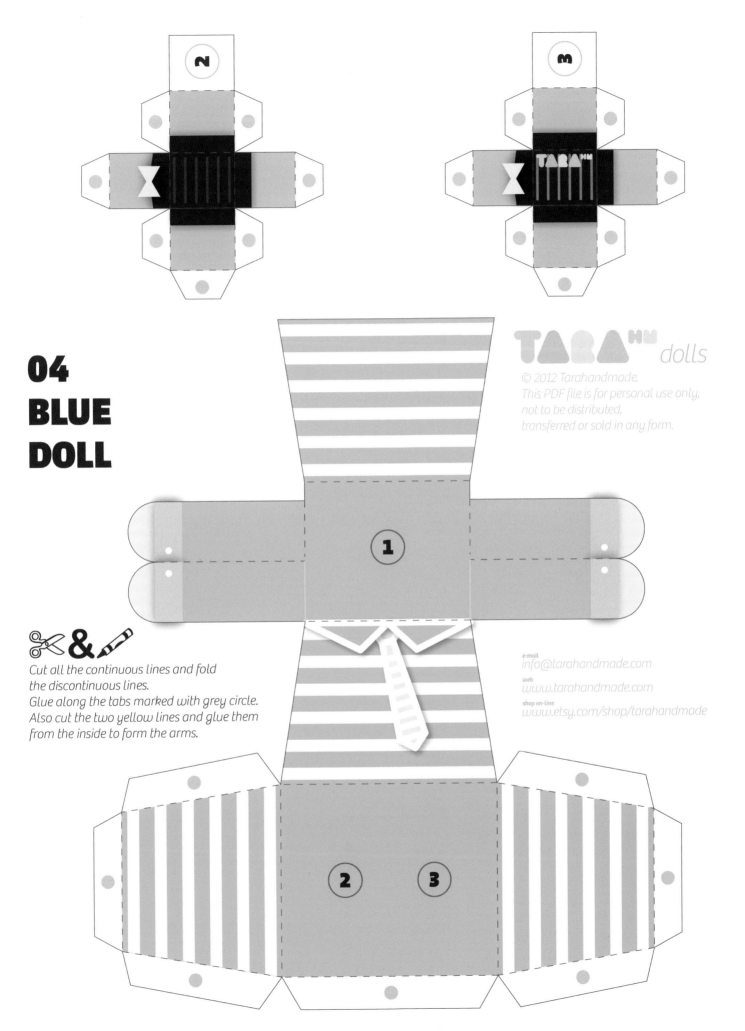

04 BLUE DOLL

TARA^{HM} *dolls*

Cut all the continuous lines and fold
the discontinuous lines.
Glue along the tabs marked with grey circle.
Also cut the two yellow lines and glue them
from the inside to form the arms.

e-mail
info@tarahandmade.com
web
www.tarahandmade.com
shop on-line
www.etsy.com/shop/tarahandmade

R ear

L ear

head ↗

FRONT

Fold

Cut

Glue

CHARACTERISTICS

STRENGTH	10 /10	INTELLIGENCE	8 /10	SOCIAL	4 /10
DEXTERITY	9 /10	WISDOM	1 /10	KAWAIINESS	5 /10

INSTRUCTIONS

1. Cut out your Pepetz with a pair or scissors (an axe can work too).
2. Fold on according to the lines separating all Pepetz faces.
3. Use some glue to stick the flaps marked "glue" and press them against the matching side.
4. Your Pepetz is alive, you can now pimp your desk.

cut in

cut in

Zerolabor Fula

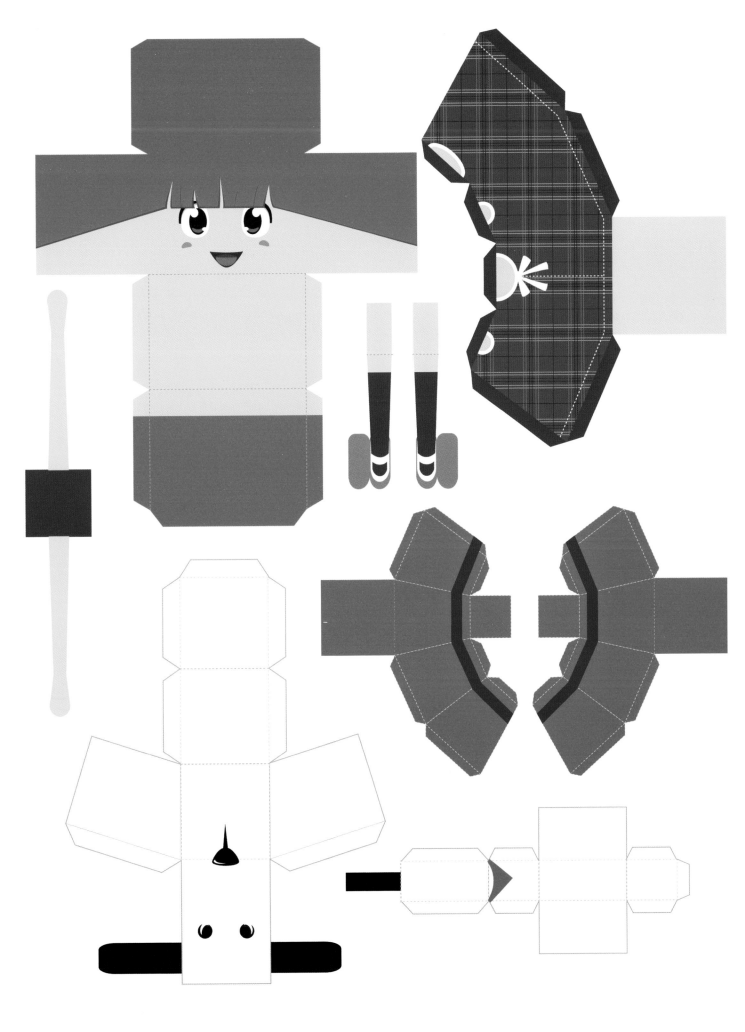

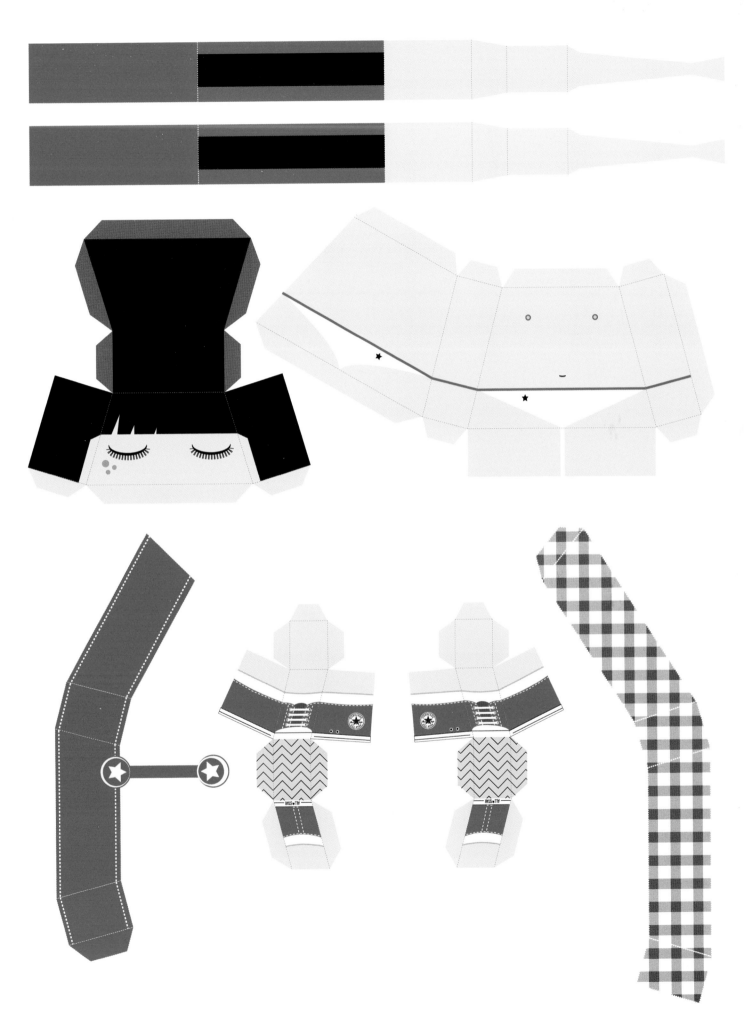

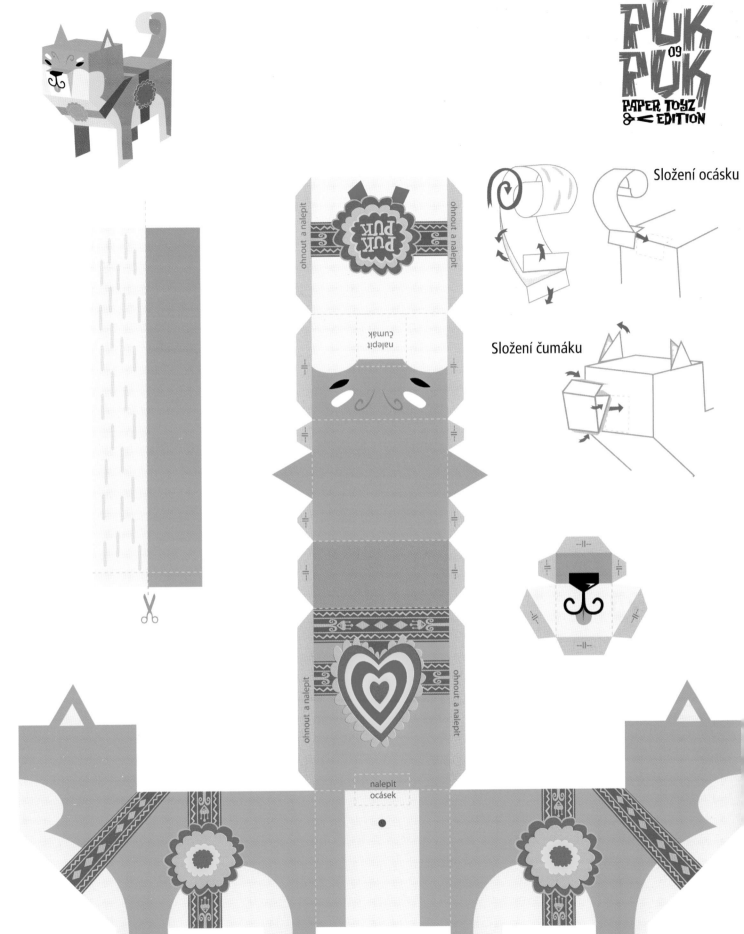

Složení ocásku

Složení čumáku

ohnout a nalepit

nalepit čumák

ohnout a nalepit

ohnout a nalepit

ohnout a nalepit

nalepit ocásek

PUK PUK
09
PAPER TOYZ
&< EDITION

PUK PUK